Gifts

Barbara Cole, Ph.D.

Gifts

*Reflections
on Receiving
and Giving*

Barbara Cole, Ph.D.

SHANTI ARTS PUBLISHING
BRUNSWICK, MAINE

Gifts

Reflections on Receiving and Giving

Published by Shanti Arts Publishing

Designed by Shanti Arts Designs

Cover image: Nito/stock.adobe.com

Shanti Arts LLC
193 Hillside Road
Brunswick, Maine 04011
shantiarts.com

Printed in the United States of America

ISBN: 978-1-956056-83-9 (softcover)

Library of Congress Control Number: 2023934298

*To those, whomever, whenever, and wherever,
who have given so much to me.*

Contents

Acknowledgements for Gifts

I AM APPRECIATIVE OF SO MANY PEOPLE WHO HAVE been helpful in making this book arrive on print or electronic bookshelves.

It goes without saying that the many who through the years have given gifts to me, wanted or unwanted, have contributed to this. Others have contributed as they have read and responded to various drafts of the book. In advance, my apologies to anyone who may have been helpful and somehow I have left your name out of this grouping.

Let me begin by thanking my childhood school chum Donna Higgins Cunningham who has always encouraged me to write, to tell my story. The San Miguel Tuesday-Wednesday Writers Group provided me with unspoken and invaluable support by setting the stage each week to show up and write.

To Mercedes Sancho, the Costa Rica lawyer who started me thinking about gift giving and receiving as she gave me her gracious gift; I thank you many times over and wish all your gifts to be exactly what you want and need.

In last name alphabetical order, others to whom

I am grateful include the following: Richard Benson, Harry Bowkley, Diana Case, Laura Celesti, Susan DuMond, Rebecca Dunlap, Stephenie Kahn, Ted Jablonski, Elizabeth May, Will Perkins, Cathy Siegner, Phyllis Smith, Kim Snyder, Richard Tortorica, Terry Schladenhauffen, Glenn Talken, Ria Talken, and the too many to list writing instructors who have guided me through the years.

I thank Publisher Christine Cote whose vision aligned with mine that Shanti Arts readers were ones most appropriate for this content as they are both significant givers and receivers.

I thank every reader of this volume. May all your gift giving and receiving experiences be perfect for you in all ways.

Keep on receiving and giving.

Barbara Cole, Ph.D.

Someone I loved once gave me a box full of darkness. It took me years to understand that this, too, was a gift.

—Mary Oliver

Gift Giving History:
When and How It Started

The greatest gift is not being afraid to question.

—Ruby Dee

EGYPTIANS ARE CREDITED WITH BEING THE FIRST in a long line of country gift givers; however, the cave crowd, long before Egypt or any place was considered a country, actually wins the prize for being first. Regardless of how I try, though, I can't quite visualize, right after fire was developed, Cave Dweller #1 approaching Cave Dweller #2, suggesting that #1 owned a stone, stick, or fuel that would be useful to #2, whereby #1 handed the item to #2. First gift given!

Maybe it happened. Maybe not.

Greeks followed the Egyptians in gift giving and receiving development. They found it enjoyable to give items, useful or not, to persons of higher authority in celebrating an event. Some historians maintain that the Greeks are the ones we must blame or eulogize for the guilt we feel if we forget someone's birthday or don't have the "right" gift for them.

By the time so-called civilization had reached the Middle Ages, gift giving between lovers had grown in popularity. Gifts might include not just an item but a poem or a love song. Dolly Parton, Bad Bunny, Frank Sinatra, or Beyonce have sung to us from a long history of love songs, gifts to one another and the public.

Even animals are in on the game. Cat lovers report that their favorite felines often show up depositing bloody prey on the doorstep. A gift to their human, perhaps a teachable moment, they think. Maybe the human will get the idea of how to find and bring home food. Other animal gift givers range from fireflies and nursery web spiders to kingfishers and gorillas. Gift giving as an enticement for sex often occurs among male fireflies and other creatures. Often the gifts, particularly nuptial ones, are nutritious and intended to encourage healthy offspring.

Crows are known to bring gifts to humans with whom they have developed a bond. Numerous examples are found, both in scientific literature and anecdotal reports of crows bringing, even creating, gifts to those who have been kind to them in some way, such as feeding or rescuing them from a dangerous situation. Candy hearts, pine sprigs laced through an aluminum soft drink can tab, keys, and earrings are among the examples of what crows are known to have been given.

Native Americans, especially those in the northwestern part of the Unites States are known to have gift giving ceremonies. The ceremonies can continue for days and focus in various ways on prestige. Items can be given away or destroyed, allowing redistribution, even regifting as some might call it, to occur.

The term "potlatch" means to give. The belief that comes with a potlatch is both a powerful and interesting one. Contrary to what many believe—that a rich person is one who retains the most—those involved in potlatch ceremonies maintain that the wealthiest and most powerful are those who give away the most. While other activities such as child naming, marriage, or mourning the dead occur at a potlatch, the belief is that One beyond us, our Creator, the Universe— however one refers to an entity beyond life on this planet—gave to us. In turn, we should give to others.

To Think About

1. If you were living in early Egyptian times, what gift do you think you might have given and to whom? Why do you say that?

2. Can you think of a time when an animal might have given you a gift, but you did not realize what was happening? What was the gift and what were the circumstances?

3. What kind of gift history does your family or did your ancestors have?

Unexpected Gifts

And you can always, always, give kindness.

—Anne Frank

COFFEE MUG IN HAND, ONE SUNNY MORNING A FEW months ago, I sauntered out my front door, eager to watch a hummingbird pecking at an orange pomegranate blossom. A young Costa Rican lawyer whom I had met the previous day, staying in the airbnb next door, passed by, struggling over the cobblestones, pulling her roll-along suitcase. I greeted her, saying I was sorry to see her go, and that I had enjoyed meeting her.

Stopping, she turned and responded with equivalent niceties to me. Suddenly, she whirled around, asking, "Would you like a sweater?" Before I could respond, she continued. "It's brand new. I just bought it before I came here. I've never worn it. The tags are still on it."

Through the years I've learned that often it is better to say yes than no, especially when someone wants to give something to you.

The lawyer continued enthusiastically. "Shopping is great here. I bought so much that I couldn't get my suitcase closed. I had to leave something, and the sweater is bulky."

"OK," I said. If it doesn't fit, I thought, I'll pass it on to someone in the community.

"Great, great. Let me go get it. I just left it in the house." In less than a minute, she returned, handing me an eye-grabbing, tangerine sorbet-colored, cropped top, thick, long-sleeved sweater. I thanked her as off she ran to catch her Uber to the airport.

I planned to pass the sweater on to someone else or donate it to a local charity. Then, on a cooler than usual day, I decided to try it on. I slipped it over my head, pulling it down to meet the black slacks I wore that day. I checked the mirror and liked what I saw. I would never have considered buying a sweater that color or style, but I liked the mirrored reflection. Maybe I'll keep it, I mused.

Now, each time I wear it, I think fondly of her and have made a donation to a charity that helps women, on her behalf.

The incident began my thinking about gift giving. Who had given me what and when through the years? To whom and what had I given? What thoughts did I have about each of these experiences?

I began to make a list of what I could remember that had been given to me and from whom. What had been my experience with the gift? Soon I had a lengthy list, and as days turned into weeks, the list grew. Memories flooded as I recalled experiences that came with those gifts. The following pages recall those gifts and include questions that I hope will help you remember the gifts you have received and also inspire ideas for future giving and receiving.

To Think About

1. What is the first gift you recall receiving? How did you feel when you received it?

2. What is the first gift you recall giving? Why did you give the gift? How do you think it was received?

3. In the preceding story, what thoughts do you think this gift giver might have had after she gave the gift to the recipient?

A Few of My Giving and Receiving Experiences

Gift giving is a true art.

—Vera Nazarian, *The Perpetual Calendar of Inspiration*

CHRISTMAS, THE MAJOR GIFT-GIVING SEASON OF the year for non-Jews, non-Muslims, and non-Buddhists, has passed. Finally.

This holiday, larger every year thanks to increased marketing efforts, has a questionable history. It is touted to be the day on which Jesus was born, but when Pope Julius I wanted to designate a day that would annually mark Jesus's birth, he took into account the Roman celebration of Saturnalia, which took place in the third week of December. Saturnalia was a time when slaves became masters, peasants were in charge, and the entire social order was turned upside down with schools and businesses closing. In addition, on December 25, many Romans celebrated Mithra, the Sun God, and it was the mot sacred day of the year. Why not designate that day as Jesus's birthday?

Whatever the true history, Christmas is a big celebratory season with gift giving a major focus.

Lucky and grateful I was this year. I received not a single gift. And fortunate I was as I felt no obligation to give any.

Run from shop to shop or visit the next online site to grab or order an item, get it wrapped, and make sure the recipient receives it on time? Not me. I've got books to read, travel documentaries to watch, recipes to try, seeds to plant, and a list of other ways I prefer to spend my time and energy.

Scrooge? Maybe. Maybe not.

I used to hate gift giving. Now, I don't enjoy it much, but I'm coping better with it.

When I feel I should give a gift—and please note this guilt-laden word "should"—and deal with all the implications that accompany it, I agonize. I procrastinate and think unpleasant thoughts about the culture that expects me to gift. I don't even like the term "to gift" that is used commonly these days. When did gift become a verb? What was wrong with the terms "give, giving, gave"? They worked for centuries.

Think this is a rant? Hang on. Bear with me.

It is not that I don't like the person for whom the gift is intended. Nor is it that I don't have funds to make a purchase. Rather, I rarely enjoy spending my time shopping for anything or anyone, including myself. Even less do I like spending time or funds shopping for someone about whom I may or may not care, for an item which they may or may not desire, and for one that could soon be useless and make little positive impact on them or the planet.

Many gifts we buy end up in landfills or, at best, thrift shops. Some consume dust or maybe recline, decades later, in the back of someone's closet, the recipient feeling guilty that they didn't want the item or don't know what to do with it. "I can't bear to part with it," they wail. Their mother, great Uncle Toby, best friend, or whomever, gave it to them. They fear that person's ghost will envelop and haunt them if they move the unwanted gift, however gently, along to someone else.

Resentment arrives, lingering for longer than I'd like, when I assume obligations to give a gift.

Now, don't get me wrong, though you could do that easily given what you've just read. I love giving gifts...when I can find the right one for the right person. For example, years ago I gave my partner a heated mattress pad, and he has commented on enjoying it night after night. It has since worn out, and I recently ordered a new one. That worked.

On the other hand, I gave a battery operated, oh-so-easy wine opener to a friend. She keeps it in her basement until she hears I'll be arriving and then gets it out. She prefers an intricate, almost ornate, Rube Goldberg-like, complicated one that I can't figure out how to use. I guess it works for her when she needs it. She drinks wine much less often than me, so ease of use is not as critical to her. Probably she would be just as happy not to have received the item that she now feels obligated to retain in case I visit once every two to ten years. That a colleague had given one to me that I cherished and thought I could hardly live without did not mean it was perfect for her.

Among the gifts that I've enjoyed giving the most have been ones like the bright red geraniums from my California house. Growing prolifically, they now bloom in several locations in Monterey County. I've snipped them and given them to friends with instructions on how to put them in the ground. Soon, voila! They have bouquet quality geraniums sprouting everywhere and they, in turn, are giving them to their friends.

Recently, I began to think about all the gifts I've received in my life and how they had or had not impacted my life. Many have impacted my life in ways I did not expect when I received them.

This morning as I sat outside near a bright red poinsettia—or *nochebuena*, as Mexicans call it—I recalled a seed and plant catalogue an acquaintance gave me decades ago. Untying the thin ribbons and removing the wrap that holiday season, I thought what a strange gift it was.

The closest at that time I'd come to gardening as an adult was to skim off a few weeds in a two-by-six-foot spot outside the front door of my Kansas City, Missouri, rented house. There I laid a "seed carpet mat" I had ordered from the Sunday newspaper insert. It promised that all one needed to do was to lay the carpet. "Water it and soon you have blooms," the shiny paper advertisement promised. Perhaps my water delivery techniques failed me. Maybe it was a too cool spring. All I know is that I saw not one bloom, not even any promises of such.

Why would anyone give a paperback the size of a coffee table book that was essentially a sales catalogue? Why would she give me that? Why would she give me any gift, given I hardly knew her? I recalled no discussions with her about plants or vegetables.

Years later I'm grateful for that gardening catalogue gift as it was the beginning of learning about beautiful blooms, such as tulip vines, the ones that hang gorgeously off fences in warm, even tropical, climates; or *Pyracantha*, known as firethorn, turning its white flowers into red berries, delighting birds each autumn. It suggested to me that other books might be available whereby I could learn how plants propagated, how they should be cared for, and even divided. Most of all, I learned how flowers, vegetables, shrubs, and trees can give immense joy.

Years passed, and Kathy, the gift giver, and I went our separate ways. She and her husband remained in the ministry. My husband and I separated and divorced, both of us leaving all connections with the church that had brought our friendship together. Sometimes I wonder if she ever remembers me or if she recalls the gift that she gave to me.

This evening my partner and I will go out dancing. Likely, I'll wrap around my neck my current favorite necklace, a gift from him, a thin silver thread with a circle displaying Oregon's mountains along with a moon or sun, depending on one's interpretation. Like life, the sun is going down or the moon is coming up, or the reverse. It matches another of my treasured gifts, a thin loose silver bracelet with seven tiny sandhill cranes hanging from it. A real treasure, I guard it jealously when I travel and never wear it if I think any possibility exists that it might be lost or stolen.

Twenty years ago, my life was in disarray. Exhaustion, resulting from a hefty schedule for my minuscule business and a flailing relationship, nearly overcame me. I had enough. I needed a break from my business, my relationship, my life. Readying my twenty-four-foot recreational vehicle, I packed my fax machine, a printer, my computer, and some clothes, and headed southeast for New Mexico.

"Good morning. Bosque del Apache Wildlife Refuge," I chirped into the phone. I had headed for Bosque Del Apache, New Mexico's impressive refuge where sandhill cranes return to their nesting spots each November. There, for most of the day at the refuge reception center, I forgot the responsibilities I had elsewhere. I accepted cash, ran credit card machines, and thanked people for coming to visit the 57,000-acre refuge. When the month was over, the staff presented me with the beautiful thin silver bracelet as a thank you gift for my volunteer efforts.

Spending time at the refuge was a gift to me, to that part of me needing space, time, and quiet. The bracelet was a gift of a different sort. Grateful I was, to say the least, for such a beautiful bracelet gift. Through the years, it has traveled with me, receiving occasional doses of anti-tarnish silver polish. The tiny cranes, dangling from its chain around my wrist, remind me of those good times. Departing the refuge, driving north on California's Highway 101, returning to a planned and hectic life, I decided to change my life. The gift became a reminder of other ways to live—to be happy, to be content.

I've been given a good life. Part of the good gifts I've been provided with by the Universe have been the opportunity and real experience to live and work throughout the world, meeting people of many cultures. Despite my best efforts, no way exists whereby I could have searched and found items to give the many people I have met who have given me so much in so many ways.

Recalling the woman who stayed with me on the Nagypur, India, train platform until she confirmed I was on the right train and in the right carriage, I am reminded of so many gifts by anonymous givers. Often the gifts were verbal as they helped me find a location I was searching for, maybe a market, an Internet café, or a jump to get my car started. Sometimes a smile and a kind look silently communicated to me became a gift.

One afternoon, running between meetings at the Karachi Sheraton after French engineers had been killed and the US Embassy bombed, I waited in a slow elevator outside my room. The door opened and a well-dressed, fine-suited Pakistani man entered. We greeted one another as the elevator descended. As we neared the lobby floor, he pleaded with me to wait. "I want to give you something" he insisted.

As I alighted and waited in the bright lobby, he hit

the up button, allowing the elevator doors to close behind him. In a few minutes, he returned with a thin hardbound volume in his hands.

"I want you to have this," he said. "I wrote it." Dubious about his motivation—I'm unaccustomed to men rushing me in the elevator with a book of poetry in their hands—I thanked him profusely and chalked it up to another of those interesting experiences one has in countries other than the US and Europe.

Years later it remains at the top of a stack of my favorite books, the ones I look at periodically to remember who I have been and, more so, who I am—a person to whom the Universe has been bountiful, providing me with numerous memorable experiences.

The lovely book of poems he authored is not the only gift I've been given by a man whom I've seen for only a few minutes and never had any previous connection with, and with whom nothing was expected as a result of the exchange. Like lots of other life experiences I cannot explain, I can't account for why the gifts were given to me. I just know the gift giving event happened.

Years ago, a job, like several I've had, called for me to spend many evenings dining alone in hotel restaurants. Unlike many people, I'm content eating alone; in fact, I rather enjoy it. It affords me the opportunity for calmness, thinking of the day's activities, planning for tomorrow, and reading, writing, or sitting in peaceful solitude.

One cold, blustery central Montana winter evening, I left the freeway, checked into a brand name motel, found my room, and relaxed for a bit before walking down the corridor to the restaurant for dinner. By the time I arrived for dinner, the restaurant was half-filled with diners. A few families, a table with jovial businessmen, and an older man wearing well-dressed cowboy attire were in various stages of perusing the menu, placing an order with the server, enjoying their food, or finishing the last bites of their meals. I ordered, received my food, having a limited exchange with the server. Cowboy man sat two booths behind me, eating his dinner alone. I may have smiled and nodded to him when I entered; otherwise, we had no communication.

As I neared the end of my dinner, saying nothing, he passed by my table, headed toward the door where he would pass through the gift shop before he exited the lobby. I assumed he was paying his bill and leaving for the evening.

Soon he returned, heading my way.

Standing next to my table, he said, "I want you to have this," handing me a large Indian head nickel paperweight. Looking up I smiled, thanking him. With that he turned, left, never for me to see him again as far as I know.

The paperweight gift, with the Native American head sculpted by James Earle Fraser and a buffalo on the opposite side, has moved with me to many locations. I rarely look at it without thinking of the brief interaction I had with this man. Why he chose me to receive this gift, any gift, I know not. Why he chose that particular item I know not. A minuscule mystery in my life, albeit a pleasant one.

These gifts were not the only unexpected ones I received.

In corporate life, I wore suits befitting board rooms in which I held meetings or made presentations. I received compliments on my attire, so I concluded that I was relatively attractive and well dressed. One day, sitting in northern California, meeting with a client and her staff, we discussed classroom assessment procedures. The client, a former school superintendent, looked across the room at me, blurting out, "I have a dress that would be perfect on you. I'll bring it next time we meet."

"OK." I smiled, unsure of why this non sequitur had occurred and continued on with business. The next time we met, sure enough, she brought the dark olive, loose, wool jersey dress with its matching leather belt, handing it to me. Again, unsure quite how to handle the gift, I thanked her and continued on with business.

At home I tried on the perfectly fitting dress, albeit it not the color or style I would choose normally. It was the beginning of me finding a new style of clothing in which I felt more comfortable, certainly more informal than my tightly structured suits. Compliments I received when I wore the dress made me rethink how good a color olive was for me. Soon I bought a two-piece olive dress, strappy olive heels...maybe I even ate more green olives.

Significant gift giving began for me in high school with a boyfriend who gave me two cashmere sweaters and a piano. The white one came with an attached lace hood, making me feel I looked like old Hollywood glamor when I wore it. When I think back on that, I am stunned by the gift. Was I that poor or was he that wealthy, I wonder? How and why did he choose to give me those items? I'll never know. Nor do I need to know.

Gift giving rarely happened in my family. One Christmas my mother explained that we had no money for gifts. She went on to engage me in thinking what we could give my sister, now living away from home. Finally, we agreed that a seventeen-cent box of Kleenex would be appropriate as my sister often sniffled and wadded up tissues. What my mother did not know is that she gave me the gift of thinking creatively and "thinking outside the box."

A box of chocolate cherries, the cheap ones you find stacked at a Walmart entrance display at Christmas, was one of only two gifts I recall my father ever giving my mother. The other gift? An Electrolux vacuum cleaner. Perhaps the new floral wool carpet installed in our living room created the need.

I was five that year, and from that day on and for many years, I took vacuum cleaners for granted. The old silver cylinder Electrolux always worked. It never failed to suck up dirt, food crumbs, pet hair, or whatever from the carpet. It never, never floundered, regardless of where I dragged it and plugged in its long cord.

Mother died and my sister inherited the vacuum cleaner. When she and her husband built a new house with a built-in vacuum system, she no longer needed the family one. I inherited it as the vacuum cleaner became another gift. I pulled it with me across carpets from Iowa to Missouri to Oregon to California. There, it stopped. It would work no more.

A vacuum cleaner was just a vacuum cleaner. Right? Surely, any vacuum would work, and I didn't want to spend the money that a new Electrolux would cost. So I bought brand after brand of vacuum cleaners, and they all worked for approximately five weeks until I or a cleaner, gave up on them, disgustedly saying they were worthless. By then the Electrolux had become so much a part of my life that I composed a story about its prowess.

I never knew Andrew Carnegie, but I wish I had. He passed through life long before I entered it, but he gave me a wonderful gift. Millions of others received the same gift. That he gave the same gift to so many doesn't make it any less significant or powerful for me. It only increases the strength of that gift.

Carnegie, the Scottish immigrant who became an American steel magnate, made his millions, now worth sixty-five billion dollars by today's standards, gave me and so many others the gift of free libraries. Yes, access to books, newspapers, and magazines at no cost to anyone who walks through the library's doors. True, taxpayers and donors contribute, but without the magnificent buildings and the encouragement Carnegie left, we would not have the more than twenty-five hundred wonderful libraries spread across the US. We might say that Carnegie reflected the Native American potlatch culture.

Growing up in one of the Carnegie-funded libraries, the one in Portsmouth, Ohio, I know how important these institutions are. My mother worked next door at the YMCA. Summers, when I went with her to her job, I spent hours next door in the library's stacks, curling up in a comfortable chair, discovering Sigmund

Freud and myriad other authors I would never have discovered otherwise in my small southern Ohio rural community.

Not only was the building filled with books and magazines, but it was filled with beauty. Its neoclassical style, built from local stone quarry materials, awed me each time I entered the doors. Above its stately hand-crafted doors, a sign read Open to All. The library's stunning domed skylight was impressive enough that in 1910, the F. W. Woolworth company published postcards that highlighted it. The Reitz Stone Company, a local one, received the contract to use local Scioto County materials in building most of the structure.

More than a century later, the building remains an impressive and useful gift to all members of the community. And the entry sign still says, Open to All.

Slicing my morning bagel or loaf of rustic bread, I think of my curly white-haired psychologist friend, Diana. She's the one who gave me the long, solid, serrated-edge bread knife I use, the one that started life in California, moved with me to Kazakhstan, Oregon, back to California, and is now in Mexico.

"Let me give you money for this beautiful knife," I said. "No, no," she replied. "It's a gift."

I explained to her that it may be a gift and I was ever so grateful for it, however, an old superstition told me that giving a knife means a cut will be made in the friendship. I valued our many years of friendship and did not want a break in the relationship. Finally, we agreed that she would accept three cents in exchange for the knife. The knife has continued to perform magnificently, and our friendship has remained intact.

Some gifts I have received have come from bosses. A favorite, lasting for decades, was a slow burning, twelve-inch, white, Christmas tree-shaped candle. Lighting the candle allowed viewers to see the wax tree glow, perfect for winter holiday settings. The boss was an older man, focused on his science education work, and I was honored to have been hired by him to coordinate a project funded by the National Science Foundation. He had even kept the job open for me until I returned to the area following a summer break. That, in itself, was a gift that added to my self-worth.

Years later, a different boss, in a different organization and halfway across the country, presented me with a surprising gift. Raised as a Catholic, he had discovered other ways to believe and had found the Siddha Yoga path with the teachings of Gurumayi. He signed me up, without asking, for a Siddha Yoga home study course. While I have not always followed her teachings, his gift brought me closer to learning and wanting to know more about Buddhist teachings.

Self-realization, the goal of the Siddha Yoga path, seems like the ultimate gift one could give oneself. My boss's gift teaching me about meditation, chanting, and contemplation has been one that has stayed with me through the years as it inspired new ways of thinking how to live one's life.

To Think About

1. What has been your gift giving history?

2. What kinds of gifts do you enjoy giving or receiving?

3. Are there any specific reasons for which you like to give or receive gifts?

4. What gifts have you been given that have brought significance to your life through the years? If so, how have they impacted your life?

Gifts Can Hurt

It's so tempting to resist a little gift when you're expecting the otherwise.

—Toba Beta, *Master of Stupidity*

GIFTS CAN HURT THE RECIPIENT. I KNOW THAT hurt, and you, too, may have experienced it.

The first time was when my mother took me to Sunday school. Children of a certain age were placed that morning where the choir usually sat. For whatever reason, we were to be given gifts that morning. All the children in the pews in front of and behind me received a book. When my name was called, I approached the podium to receive my gift. Handing me a coloring book, appropriate for a child several years younger than me and who could not read, the choir leader barely acknowledged me.

A coloring book?

Tears stung. Did this man handing me the book not think I could read? I was in the fourth grade and read every book I could get my hands on. My self-worth plummeted. Did he know something about me I did not? Was I not worthy of a book with regular words in it like the others had received?

How silly it seems now, but when you feel singled out for something negative you don't understand, the salty weeps come easily. I'm sure the man at the pulpit was only trying to keep the service running smoothly, perhaps ran out of age-appropriate books when my turn came but didn't want me to leave with nothing in my hands. Irrational to be hurt about it, but it left an impression.

Such is life.

Decades later, a man I thought was the love of my life and who loved history gave me a beautiful thick hardcover book, *The Timetables of History*, a timeline of the world. Impressed I was until I read the inscription that said something about us being apart but remembering history.

Really? Remembering history? Hmmm.

The message was clear. He had no plans that we would always be together. It could have been written to a colleague or someone whom he had seen in passing in a restaurant and would never see again. It was not the written gesture of someone with whom one had loved, traveled, worked, and owned property—together.

Together? The gift said otherwise.

Another gift I received brought a painful message as well. Yes, another love but he, too, had chosen someone else with whom to share his time. Perhaps trying to remain friends, he invited me to breakfast for my birthday. Driving us down the Big Sur Coast, we dined at a charming, woodsy, even romantic restaurant I'd heard about and always wanted to visit.

The restaurant lived up to its fame. It was cozy and cleverly presented, having hosted numerous celebrities through the years. With a fireplace's flames roaring near our table, we caught up on what we had been doing since we last saw one another, carefully avoiding certain topics. I inquired about his parents and his children. He inquired about my recreational vehicle that I'd bought for business and pleasure, which I had named Clarence, for no particular reason.

Clarence and I had experienced several adventures in the previous few years, too complex to enunciate here. I'd taken Clarence, comfortable as he was, with me on more than one road trip during which I had to be towed miles to a repair shop. Clarence's brakes had gone out on a Sierra high mountainous road, and only the grace of many gods had gotten me safely stopped on flatter ground.

As breakfast ended, my former lover reached under his seat and brought out a medium-sized box wrapped in gold with a proper red bow. "Happy Birthday," he said as he checked his watch. Ahh, I thought. He has a date with the new girlfriend and needs to be sure he can make the drive back to town in time.

He put the box on the table in front of me, and I began to untie the ribbon. "I hope you will enjoy this," he said nonchalantly.

Pulling off the wrapping paper, I discovered that I was being given a CB radio. Had I ever once exhibited any verbal or nonverbal desire for one of the loud, crackling, dreadful sounding devices long distance truckers use to connect with one another? "Trucker, trucker . . ."

Never.

In retrospect, I suppose I should give the guy credit for thinking that given my RV mishaps before the days of cell phone coverage, a CB radio was a great idea for someone who might need to get help should my car break down in a remote area. Years passed with me never opening or using the item. While I might have found it useful, it was distasteful to me, but more so, the message it gave was excruciatingly painful: "I won't be with you to help with this or anything else." The message hurt. I was accustomed to taking care of myself in all ways; however, during the years of this relationship, I'd come to think that I might have someone on whom I could rely for at least a few things. Now I knew that no possibility for such existed.

I was all alone again, but I did not yet know what a gift aloneness could be. Only years later did I unwrap that wonderful gift of aloneness as I discovered how much more productive, happy, and content I could be in my solitude.

Occasionally—probably more than occasionally—I have been given items that I did not want. Haven't we all? Receiving a gift means that someone has spent at least a bit of time thinking about what I might want or need. They had gone to some trouble to acquire it and then put it in a form to present to me. But those actions did not mean I was ready to appreciate the gift.

Now I was faced with what to do with unwanted or unexpected gift.

One such example is a troll doll, not the kind that became popular in the sixties but one coming from Norwegian folklore. These handcrafted wooden dolls are created in varying degrees of ugliness, their major feature being a huge crooked nose. The dolls supposedly live under bridges and have witch-like capabilities; their wrinkled faces can frighten anyone who sees them.

Holiday behaviors in organizational settings often create innumerable problems, yet they are ones that few dare to discuss. Most put on their happy faces and go along with the crowd. Rarely was my own situation different.

Corporate settings are great places for game playing. Trainers use games to discover who are the most competitive employees or to teach a particular skill set. I'm neither very competitive nor fond of playing games, preferring to spend time in a multitude of other ways.

One year our department in the corporation where I worked was informed by the senior manager's staff assistant that our group would be holding a combination of Secret Santa and White Elephant exchanges at the annual Christmas luncheon. Never mind that a staff member might not celebrate the holidays. At some point she came around, insisting that each of us pull a slip of paper from an oversized hat. The slip of paper had the name of the person for whom we would be a Secret Santa.

Exhausted and overwhelmed with work before this announcement arrived, I groaned at having another task on my list—to find a gift item with humor attached to it to give to the person for whom I was a Secret Santa. Buying a White Elephant gift felt like only perpetuating kitsch and clutter.

The day of the luncheon we gathered at a nearby restaurant, everyone trying to be on his/her best behavior given that top management was present. Following a couple of drinks and food, festivities began. The assistant, a middle-aged woman with a British accent who everyone disliked as she lorded it over everyone except her boss, had gathered all the gifts along with the names of the recipients but not the givers—that was to remain secret. To make matters more complex, if a person didn't like the gift they received, they could pass it on to someone else.

Whatever I gave to the person whose name I had drawn was not been received with great enthusiasm. My gift to them? A donation to the local animal shelter. Not much humor, but a way to send a message about the need to care for unwanted animals. Too esoteric or whatever for this crowd, I learned.

Receiving my gift from the person who had drawn my name, I smiled as best as I could, thanking them and accepting it. The gift? An ugly, ugly troll doll with a huge, bulbous nose and wrinkled face. Fighting back the tears, I rewrapped it and put it aside, trying to continue with the party festivities. Yes, I could have passed it onward but why would I want to give such a gift to another? To another participant, this gift may have been humorous but not to me in my emotionally fragile state.

Teased by my sixth grade classmates about the bump in my nose, I determined that the first money I made as an adult would be dedicated to having rhinoplasty to remove the bump. I recalled my shock when I first visited Italy, riding inner-city buses, discovering how many women on the bus had noses identical to mine. Did I have Italian ancestry? Not to my knowledge, yet they looked so much like me. I continued to wonder how it could be that we could look so much alike when they didn't speak English. Ah, how much I had to learn.

The despicable troll doll felt like a hurtful stab at me from a coworker, though I knew not who. My job in the company was one that often called on me to challenge staff. The company had been producing certain products in a specific manner. They were perfect for a time gone by but not for the current and future times. When the company acquired a project to produce a modified product in a period of months, not years, it was my responsibility to keep people on task. One person yelled at me, "Barbara, stop trying to make us stay on schedule!" Hmmm.

I did not relent and tried to work with them, keeping the client, the company higher-ups, and the employees happy. My gift to myself was only more stress.

If humiliating me with the gift was the plan, whoever gave me the doll succeeded as I retreated from the luncheon in tears. Sadness about knowing I'd be spending the upcoming holidays alone was not lessened by the gift. The event remained hurtful for weeks and did nothing to encourage my gift giving or receiving for years. I may have been a bit too tender-skinned, but it hurt.

To Think About

1. Have you ever received a gift that you found to be insulting or hurtful? What about the gift made you feel that way? Was it related to the person who gave it to you? Or to the setting?

2. Have you ever given a gift that you later realized may not have been appropriate and could have hurt the recipients?

Diverse, Intangible, Even Unknown to Givers and Receivers

Cease to inquire what the future has in store and take as a gift whatever the day brings forth.

—Horace

*A*S I'VE WRITTEN ELSEWHERE, I ENJOY DINING alone, especially when I can sit at a white table-clothed location, have food more delicious than I could prepare, and a server who is not doting but conscious of my taste and drink needs. I can listen to someone else's life, live a few minutes of it, and then continue with mine, the one I'm grateful to have received.

Completing my doctorate at the University of Oregon, I worked on campus on various projects. Eugene, at that time, had few restaurants other than fast food. My research assistant status allowed me to dine in the university's faculty dining room. I was thankful for the opportunity to walk across the leafy campus, climb the steps to the old historic, now preserved Victorian-style Collier House. There I sat alone, contemplating my current projects and future career. How should I handle the issues I was grappling with on my dissertation? When I interviewed faculty members who had been participants in the organization I was studying, I knew if I told the truth in my dissertation, it would not be well received, even by some of my committee members. To not tell the truth was unthinkable. How would I work it out?

I fretted about finding a job when I completed my degree. Where would I go? What would I do?

Over vichyssoise and salad, I pondered my troublesome love (or the lack thereof) life. I'd had what I considered my first life failure—my marriage.

On and on I muddled and wrestled with life issues, but there, in the quiet, stately dining room, I had the gift of calmness, serenity, grace.

A lovely gift, even a much needed gift to myself.

Sometimes folks give us gifts, and neither the receiver nor the giver understands fully the gifts that are being given. A major one that comes to mind for me is a room in a beautiful house, even a home. Let me explain.

Two little girls, one five and the other six, met in their first-grade classroom. Decades later, they attend one another's major birthday parties, email each other, and remain connected to events occurring in one another's lives. One has deep family roots, while the other has broad friendship tendrils reaching around the world. They may not finish one another's sentences, but they both know the southern Ohio culture from which they came. The one with the deep family roots is my friend Donna. The other is me.

Often she has told me "to come home". For years I've considered my home to be thousands of miles from her house which is near where we grew up, yet her welcoming attitude has subtly encouraged me to return to that area far more frequently than I would have otherwise.

Recently, exhausted from a spat with my live-in partner, I found myself thinking of the room she has so welcomingly provided when I've visited her. Sleeping alone on a comfortable bed under downy sheets and an old-fashioned quilt, a tiny fresh bedside table bouquet, family photos, sheer curtains wavering in the breeze of the overhead fan felt just right. Perhaps I wanted to retreat to her basement family room, festooned with family photos, a fireplace, comfortable seating space, but most of all, good energy. Safe, quiet energy, the kind I longed for, protected from outside, distracting elements.

Isn't that what home is supposed to provide? Quite a gift, I'd say.

Despite the snow and bitterly cold winds present in November, I thought of booking a ticket to take advantage of the gift, even holing up alone there over the Thanksgiving holidays while she joined her family elsewhere. Just me and the quiet. Ultimately, I did not go, didn't even suggest to her or anyone else that I considered it, but I knew the gift was there.

That's what made the difference. Just knowing the gift was available.

To Think About

1. What gifts have you given yourself? Did you think about why you wanted them before you acquired them? Did the gifts give you what you hoped to receive?

2. What gifts do you plan to give yourself in the future? Do you know why you want that particular item or experience?

Forgetting What We've Given

*The greatest gift you can ever give another
person is your own happiness.*

—Esther and Jerry Hicks

O CCASIONALLY I FORGET A GIFT I'VE GIVEN. ASIDE
from a slight concern about absent-mindedness, I
confess I like that about myself. Some givers hold
on to what they've given someone, wanting that person
to be beholden to them or always expressing their
gratitude for the gift. I don't want to be one of those.

On one of Monterey's foggy evenings, having been
invited for dinner at her hilltop house, I walked into my
friend Beth's beautifully redone kitchen. The contractor
she had hired and to whom she had given a huge down
payment had walked out on her, filed bankruptcy, and
left her house with a wide gaping hole, previously
known as her kitchen. She—clever, creative, and the
artist she is—completed it by herself. Stunningly well
designed and constructed, a credit to her talents, it
was. I was pleased to be there.

Gaping in amazement at her workmanship, I gasped to see an artistically designed, clear glass object on the countertop. Abstract and a most unusual design, it was simply gorgeous, an attention-grabbing object in any setting.

"Beth, wherever did you get that?" I exclaimed. "It is absolutely spectacular," I gushed.

"You gave it to me!" she replied. "I really like it too."

To this day I do not recall buying or giving the gift, but I'm glad I did. If I did. Beth says I did, and I'm happy to believe her. I'm happy to accept the gratitude for it.

Years later she gave me a small, white, elongated dish with three tiny white ceramic bowls fitting within it, perfect for dipping sauces—the kind of item that I would never have bought for myself, considering it far too frivolous. Surely, I could "make-do" with other small dishes I had, I'd tell myself and pass it on the shelf, even a sale rack.

Now it sits above a kitchen bar where I use the gift every day. While it has held dipping sauces and marmalades, most frequently, it holds three fresh small lemons I've gathered from the ground where they have fallen, just outside my Mexican kitchen's large window. They grace the kitchen with charm I would never have expected and yes, often when I admire them, I am thankful for Beth and our many years of enduring friendship. I consider the lemons a gift from another source, one that gives and gives as the rains replenish the tree's energies.

Beth arrived late one weekday morning at my house. Responding to an ad I had placed, she looked around, first at the room that would be hers if she rented. Then she toured the rest of the house that I chose to show to prospective tenants lest they wonder about it and who lived in the other wing. We stood near the entrance in the foyer as she said she'd let me know if she wanted to live there.

Days, even a couple of weeks passed before I heard from her. My schedule was such that I didn't get around to interviewing anyone else. I don't recall that anyone else showed up who was of interest to me. Later she contacted me and came to live there for several years.

When the two-bedroom guest house became vacant, she moved into it, then rented the second bedroom to a woman. At some point, Beth's teenage niece joined her there. Eventually Beth moved into Carmel with a man who had worked for me for a few days on a set of writing assessment projects I was overseeing. I rented the guest house and the extra room to other people and life continued.

Eventually I—without a relationship and without anyone living in the guest room, maybe I was going away again, traveling for an extended time period— decided to rent the room again. I placed an ad, but at the same time, I ran into a friend of hers and mentioned I had just placed an ad. Beth called me and soon she was back "home" where she had been years before.

She lived there until she bought her own place in town. We saw one another occasionally but overall, we had separate lives. The gift of our friendship continues.

I'm not alone in forgetting what I've given. Recently, I thanked a friend for the second audiobook she had given me within a month. "I sent you another book?" she questioned. She went on to say that she had set up some automatic gifts for year's end but had forgotten what she had given to me and to another friend. Sometimes we are overwhelmed with life, zoning out as we try to manage life events. Giving to another should not add more stress to our lives.

Perhaps more significant is when we forget what we've been given. Often we have been given gifts, by design or happenstance, that we fail to recognize. "Taking it for granted" is a phrase we hear sometimes when someone says they or someone about whom they are talking ignored the opportunity or gift they had been given. The person had behaved as if they expected the gift with more to come without giving anything in exchange.

Gifts are free. That's a major part of the definition of a gift. Free, no strings attached. Often advertisements will include a blurb saying, "free gift." No. That's not a gift. That's merely an enticement for the purchaser to exchange resources for the advertised product or service and other items, but it is not a gift.

Many in developed countries have little awareness of the gifts they were given at birth, from clean water and clean air to education and more. We expect these, yet, they are gifts to us.

Sometimes the gifts we are given are not always ones we want. As Mary Oliver declared in her oft-quoted line, years may need to pass before we become aware of how awesome the gift was, how much it benefited us, how much we learned from it, or how it kept us from making a dreadful life-impacting error.

Emotional pain can be affiliated with the gift. Recalling the gift but not the pain affiliated with it may be the more recent challenge we face. Remembering the gift of not getting the promotion but not the agony or embarrassment we might have felt at the time may move us emotionally to locations we do not wish to visit. Sometimes we need to remember that the gift of loss when our lover rejected us saved us from years of anguish when the lover turned out to have addiction or criminal issues.

Gratitude lists have become popular in the last two decades. Oprah swears by them as do many others. Berne Brown laughs at herself, trying to give gratitude in the middle of upsetting circumstances. Often, making such a list is prescribed to folk bemoaning a recent loss or complaining about a life circumstance not to their liking, saying they have nothing for which they can be grateful. Yet as those same people focus on what they have instead of what they have lost, often they discover more of what is better for them and what they want comes to them.

Starting with the simplest and often overlooked item such as the air we breathe and our ability to breathe it, gratitude lists have no limit. They can include numerous items we have forgotten or take for granted even though we have received those items, whereby tremendous good comes to us.

To Think About

1. What gifts have you been given that you took for granted, not acknowledging to yourself or others that they were gifts? What have you done with those gifts?

2. What's on your gratitude list? What else might you add?

3. What did you once think was dreadful but now you are so grateful to have received it?

Gift Superstitions

*The best gift is one that benefits
both the receiver and the planet.*

—Andrew Weil, MD

*A*S IF GIFT GIVING WERE NOT WEARISOME ENOUGH, at least for people like me, it becomes even more complex when you read or hear about all the superstitions that come along with it. For example, giving a container of parsley to a friend whom you know loves to garden and cook seems like a perfect gift. Not so fast! Through the years, some folks (and who they are and what their research is, I do not know) have said that parsley should never be given.

Why? you ask. Sounded like a great idea, especially if you have a bountiful, overflowing garden.

Whoever the "someone" was maintained that parsley, given its difficulty germinating, needed to be planted in three sowings. Two plantings were for the devil and one for the gardener.

Hmmm. I've never considered planting or doing anything for the devil, but now I know I should just plant my own parsley and let my friend "steal" it from me.

Perhaps the guidance about not being given emeralds or opals is correct. A man once gave me an opal and an emerald ring, but we went our separate ways. Turquoise and coral have their problems, too, when given as jewelry.

You read my experience earlier about receiving the gift of a knife from a friend and how we reconciled that so our friendship would not be broken by any back luck coming from the gift. Now I'm worrying about the lovely, warm pair of black cashmere gloves a different friend gave me a few years ago, a portent of a fight. Not what I want as I value her friendship. I've given her cut flowers but now I'm going to tell her that if I do that again, she should not thank me, as the thanking process could bring bad luck. Through the years she has given me a many gifts, and our friendship has endured. So I'm hoping it will continue, should I make a gifting error. I'm unsure if the bad luck might come to her or to me, but I want to take no chances with either possibility. And I think I'll just stick to giving yellow flowers as that gift brings money. Seems like a much better option for both of us.

Another list of "no-no's" for gift giving includes mirrors, empty wallets, clocks, calendars, watches, and anything sharp. Even giving an item with the wrong number can be hazardous in the gifting process.

More evidence for why I don't like this gift giving activity much. It gets complicated.

Maybe I'll just buy stock in a candy company and give sweets. Oh, no, that won't work. Most people I know these days believe sugar is bad for them, so they would regift my gift. If they believe in feng shui, that would present a dilemma for them as regifting (covered elsewhere in this book) means you are giving away the friendship with the one who gave it to you. So much for that idea.

Combs are on the not-to-give list. Years ago, I received a lovely wooden comb from a Chinese friend. We remain friends and as far as I know, no misfortune has come to either of us as a result of the gift but then, I don't know all the details in her life.

By the time I finished trying to figure out what should and should not be given, I was ready to give myself a gift. I have not discovered it but probably someone has put together a list of gifts that we should not give ourselves. Pretty sure you can't go wrong with giving yourself the gift of time, the gift of meditation, the gift of self-love.

I'll go with those.

To Think About

1. In the future, how will you handle being given something you think may create bad luck for you?

2. Can you create your own luck with the gifts you give yourself?

Gift Giving in Other Cultures

*For humans, gift giving is a universal ritual
laden with evolutionary implications.*

—Gad Saad, *The Evolutionary Bases of Consumption*

WHEN I SHARED WITH A FRIEND AND WRITING COL-
league that I was writing this book, she shared
her own gift-learning experience with me.

As a new Mexican bride to her Italian husband, she
wanted very much to make a good impression on his
friends and relatives. She's an elegant woman, but she
had no experience with being expected to take a gift
when she went to anyone's house for dinner or an event.
Her husband had said nothing about such a cultural
requirement. Off she went to an evening event, excited
to be included in the festivities. Only after she arrived
at the host's house did she discover that she was the
only one who had not brought a gift. Her mortification
did not end there, nor did it stop with chastisement
from her mother-in-law. The error of her ways, she
maintains, has remained with her through the years as

few in the community have forgotten about her lack of gift knowledge, making them wonder about what else she did not know.

Having traveled to dozens of countries and lived in seven countries besides my home country of the United States, I have had the opportunity to observe gift giving in a variety of settings. In the US, as a bride and groom prepare to marry, often they register at a local department store, but in online times, they register with Amazon or a bridal registry site such as Zola or Myregistry.com. They choose dinnerware, silverware, cooking equipment and utensils and whatever else they think they require to start a household. That makes it easy for givers, purchasing something they know the recipients desire.

Gifts can arrive at the giver's residence already wrapped, or the items can go directly to the ultimate recipient's location. The givers can attend the wedding, grateful they do not have to schlep along any packages, especially if they are traveling by air. The givers / guests can attend the function, have a drink, dance, and go on their way, having wished the newlyweds well on their intended lifetime journey.

That's not quite the way it is in Kazakhstan.

Invited to the wedding of a young woman assistant who had worked for me for several months, I was eager to attend but unsure what to expect. The wedding was in a town approximately six hours from the university that was not an easy train ride on the steppe. I had a car, so I offered to take another professor, his wife, and their two children.

The bride, resplendent in her white, western style

wedding dress, radiated happiness as did the groom and the guests as we gathered in a hall handling a couple hundred guests. Seated at a round table with seven other guests, I was asked to "head" the table, likely due to my age and employment position with the bride. In the center of the table sat the wedding yurt, white with blue and gold trim. For those unfamiliar with the concept, a wedding yurt is a miniature version of the large, heavy felt structure that can be disassembled and moved easily from one location to another on Kazakhstan's vast wind-swept steppes. Kazakh nomads have lived in the large ones, moving their herds from location to location for centuries.

Celebratory dancers lifted their feet to the loud music as servers, on their shoulders, carried huge trays of roasted horse meat, potatoes, Kazakhstan's national dish, and besbharmak, the country's staple. That's when I was informed that my duties included lifting the lid on the miniature yurt, reaching inside it, retrieving an item inside it and giving it to another guest at the table.

The pressure was on.

I had met the other guests only moments before the dancing began. I felt awkward and uncomfortable with such a task, wishing I could just sit there quietly, fade into the background, and rest before my long drive home. Trinkets of varying sorts were inside the yurt. I distributed gifts until finally, everyone had a gift and they refused to receive any more. As I prepared to exit, the bride's friends, managing the event, insisted I take the yurt with me, including all the remaining contents. Never had I left a wedding with a gift—in fact, numerous gifts. Not only did I leave with that gift, but like all other guests, I was handed a package of wedding food to take home with me, a Kazakhstani tradition, I discovered. Later I learned that the tradition of everyone receiving a gift occurs not only in Kazakhstan but in many other countries in that region, including Russia.

Weeks later, I regifted the wedding yurt, giving it to a former adult management student who had become a friend on the occasion of her marriage. I'm sure the happy couple had little idea what to do with the gift and mostly likely regifted it too.

Before going to China to work, I read as much as I could about cultural expectations there. In the US, if I were going to a friend's house, I might grab a bottle of wine or pick up some flowers. Not so easy in Shanghai or Kunming where wine drinkers are few. Choosing flowers, also not easy to find on a Chinese street, and especially white ones might mean I wished death for the recipient, a message I definitely did not want to convey. Gift items in blue, black, or white would not be well received; most gifts would be wrapped in red. Money gifts would be placed in small red envelopes. I, the university I represented, and my country would be judged by the gift I presented.

People in few countries wrap or present gifts more illustratively and beautifully than those in Japan. Knowing how perfectly designed and operationalized Japanese packages are, whether it be a toy car, a Haruki Murakami book, or a bento box filled with delectable items ready to eat, I have been thankful I have not had to meet the competitive challenge that would come with gift giving there.

A gift I love to give when I can do it with honesty

and integrity is to complement someone on something they have done, said, are wearing, or possess. Through the years, I have learned to be more careful about spurting out my complements if they are about items. The reason? Some cultures, including those in the Middle East tend to feel they should give the item to you if you complement them about it.

I may complement a woman about a high quality black abaya she is wearing; however, given my culture and the places I visit, it is unlikely I would have reason to wear it, should she give it to me. To accept the gift, especially from a giver who had limited resources would make me feel I had taken what I should not.

American businessmen are accustomed to grabbing a bottle of Scotch or an aged wine to give in a business setting. This is inappropriate in Afghanistan or elsewhere where liquor is forbidden or is not consumed due to religion reasons. Several books and websites are available to provide the specifics for such situations.

Early in the United States, especially in western communities, families had to provide food and housing for teachers in the farming and ranching outposts. Apples were among the food staples presented to the teachers—frequently, single young women. The apple became a symbol of a teacher's gift from her students.

I do not recall, as a teacher, being given gifts until I began to have more students from other countries where it is more common to give teachers gifts, sometimes in exchange for better grades. It never occurred to me to alter a grade based on a gift or that anyone would think I would. However, I discovered that some students believed such would happen given the cultural setting from which they had come. If I were in that same situation again, I would announce at the beginning of every class term that no gifts would be accepted. Period.

While I am grateful for the beautiful small wooden box with mother of pearl inlays from Syria, the freshwater pearl necklace from the Philippines, even the delicious Turkish baklava, I would not accept them again. At the time I received the items, I was trying to be encouraging to the student, welcoming them to the country, acknowledging their culture, and being supportive of them in higher education. Now I'd handle the situation in a different manner.

To Think About

1. Have you ever received a gift that you felt brought good or bad luck to you? What were your experiences?

2. Have you ever given a gift that you later realized could have been considered insulting or inappropriate to give? What happened?

3. Have you ever received a gift from someone of another culture or country that you found surprising? How did you handle the situation, and would you handle it the same way if the gift giving occurred today?

Gift Wrapping and Other Annoying Gift Issues

A wonderful gift may not be wrapped as you expect.

—Jonathan Lockwood Huie

AT TIMES, I'VE FOUND ITEMS THAT I THOUGHT would be perfect items for someone. "Whew," I would sigh with relief, assuring myself I had one more task off my to-do list. Unfortunately, not so fast, I'd discover. I would have bought the gifts, taken them home, stowed them somewhere, likely a hall closet, and they would wait for the appropriate time to give the gift. When the time came to give the gift, the item was nowhere to be found. I have "lost" innumerable gifts, some of which I've found long after they should have been given or when the person has accepted the same gift from someone else.

Is this a less than subtle but subconscious way of reminding myself how much I do not like gift giving?

Then there is the whole annoyance of gift wrapping. You buy a gift. Then you have to wrap it. You have to not just wrap it in any kind of paper but one that is appropriate for the occasion—birthday, holiday, event. Few shops have gift wrap corners these days, so you are left with doing the wrapping yourself. That means going to a location that sells wrapping paper, buying it, using it, and then storing it. I won't even mention the embarrassment if you can't get the corners squared away, a sharp corner tears the thin tissue paper, or the bow looks like a kindergartner might have used it to practice tying shoelaces.

Finally, you get it done, beginning to think about how you might hide your gift under the other wedding gifts so no one will notice the amateur job. That done, you discover that around you are scattered the bits and bobs of gift wrapping, including leftover gift paper. Surely, you will use the wrap again, you tell yourself.

Fold it, pack it, keep it.

Not so fast.

Somehow, my experience—and maybe it is just me—tells me that the next occasion always calls for some wrap that I don't have. Maybe the original wrap got damaged, or it just doesn't look right. More likely, it broadcasts "Happy Birthday," and I'm giving a graduation or retirement gift.

Usually, I buy generic wrapping paper that fits with any occasion. Same with bows. But occasionally, I get sucked into buying what is not usable for a second occasion, and then I'm stuck with the leftovers. I hate wasting anything, but sometimes it happens. Usually it goes into the waste bin when I'm doing a major cleaning, the kind of cleaning splurge that does not happen often at my house, so the paper or bows languish in the back of the closet for years.

Why has someone not (or perhaps they have) organized a gift paper and ribbon recycling post, sort of like the little free libraries that have popped up all over the country? People drop off their books and pick up another one to their liking. All free. The same could be done for gift wraps, making Marie Kondo all the prouder of the community whose closets are now de-cluttered from gift wrap.

Last year I encouraged Facebook gift givers to use newspaper, fabric, any item that they could recycle for wrapping gifts. To my surprise, more people "liked" it than any other posting I have made in years.

Then there is the matter of wrapping the gift itself, especially awkward ones. We want the gift to look as if Martha Stewart wrapped it. Mine, too often, look as if Big Bird put forth his best effort, beak and feathers included. It's enough to make me want to hide the gift under the others and placed there when no one is looking.

One year I gave up, simply gave up. I could not deal with the whole process anymore, regardless of how much I adored my friends and wanted to be included in their holiday gift exchange. To understand this fully, know that one of these friends is an artist. All of her gift items are interesting and unusual and are wrapped in clever ways.

A second friend is the epitome of glamour and elegance. Even a container of compost (a most unlikely gift for her to purchase) would be wrapped as splendidly as if Tiffany & Co. had designed, displayed, and wrapped it. Furthermore, the gift would be something you had never thought of getting for yourself, but now that she has given it to you, you wonder how you lived without it for so long.

One year all this gift giving frenzy came to a head. I just couldn't get it together with either appropriate gifts or with any kind of reasonable wrap for whatever I had found. I gave up. I dumped items I hoped people would enjoy but felt no assurance about into a large black, plastic, albeit clean (never used) garbage bag, tied it with a huge red ribbon and called it happy holidays!

That was it! *Fini! Finito! Terminado!* Finished, I was! Enough of this, I said to myself.

Arriving on the hosting friend's doorstep for the annual holiday gift exchange, I towed my two unwieldy, black, plastic albeit clean garbage bags, tied with bright red bows, in hand. Inside were the gifts to my friends. By evening's end, they had given me lovely gifts, but best of all, they'd given me the gift of tolerance for my bohemian demeanor. Gifts of love and tolerance are always welcome.

Jewelry is a gift that men often give to women as evidence of their undying love for them. Diamonds, such as the 69-carat diamond Richard Burton gave to Elizabeth Taylor, sometimes end up being the tie that binds in divorce court, not in ongoing love and affection. I've never been given a diamond by a man, only an opal and an emerald.

In the nineteen-eighties, when over-the-top exhibitions of wealth were flaunted by the many, fueled by television's *Dallas*, I began to think about how I'd like to have a man give me a gorgeous diamond. Not a run of the mill diamond ring but a really well designed, splurgy, splashy one, one that would look great on my left hand third finger as I stretched my palm, manicured fingernails or not. I wanted people to respect me because they admired my ring, thinking I must be impressive if my ring was.

Really? How shallow, I chastise myself now.

Such rings usually come with a price, dollars for the man and too often a lifetime of unwanted results for the woman. Specifically, they usually mean marriage, and I never wanted that. Even if a man had wanted to give me such a ring, I am positive I would have declined. I wanted the ring, I wanted to be wanted in marriage, but I did not want the marriage itself. Way too confining for me.

I've heard that some women have increased their fortunes by accepting expensive jewelry from men for whom they had little caring. Never been my style. Accepting a drink from a stranger has been a challenge for me to accept.

After I accepted my husband's proposal of marriage, the night I returned from my mother's funeral, I realized that we would be expected to have rings as evidence of our marriage. At some point it occurred to me, that I should have an engagement ring, but I also realized that it was unlikely he could afford to present me with such. That seemed to be OK with me then, and I thought not too much about it. Low expectations I had.

As we prepared for our wedding day, I insisted that our wedding rings be designed in a floral pattern.

Giving the jeweler a picture showing the design we wanted did not produce the desired result.

I recalled some of this years later while sitting in the boardroom of a nonprofit organization. Around the historic table sat nearly two dozen older women, trying to develop a new plan to fund the organization. Few of the women looked very healthy or attractive, I thought. Many of them looked disheveled, not smartly or interestingly dressed, but wrinkled hands displayed huge diamonds, sparkling as they turned pages in the annual report.

I puzzled this. How could they be so unattractive and yet garner such impressive jewelry? Had they purchased it themselves? Inherited it? Possibly, but unlikely, I thought.

I mentioned my surprise at these adornments to a couple of friends who set me straight as to how this had likely happened. They maintained that most women they knew who exhibited diamonds like those acquired them following the divulgement of their male spouse having an affair. The man felt guilty and didn't want a financially and emotionally costly divorce, so some form of appeasement was acquired by giving his wife a new and larger diamond. Given some of the hands I saw around the old table, I could only conclude local jewelers must have been quite busy through the years.

Years later, when I completed a consulting project in Los Angeles, I stopped in the hotel's gift shop where I was staying. There I bought a huge fake diamond, one that has spent most of its life with me, resting comfortably in a hanging jewelry container. Way too flashy for life in outdoorsy Oregon or even central or northern California, and not at all appropriate in the developing countries through which I preferred to travel. It waits. In Kazakhstan, where sequins and flash are worn commonly, occasionally, the ring would escort me to a party.

My gift to myself. A real one? Don't think so. Too much jewelry I have owned has walked away from me with me having no knowledge of where, when, or with whom it went. Now I have no interest in owning more, especially as I have learned what happens in the South African and diamond mines from which most diamonds in the US come. One of the few times when fake, even when it is a gift to oneself, is better than real.

Too often we don't give ourselves the very thing we want because we think we are unworthy of such. Can we not love ourselves, making us love others, without moving into selfish, narcissistic, behavior patterns? Surely, we can.

Sometimes, giving to oneself takes few resources. A bouquet of roses, an hour alone reading, a new gardening tool—even a secondhand one—can replenish our soul's energy, whereby we have increased energy for augmenting our family's income, tolerating habits of our teens or incompetent bosses, or creating a long-desired project.

Long before mental health days were a phrase and a possibility, I took a day away from the office. I was not physically ill, but I could not bear to spend one more hour sitting at a dull desk job redoing budgets, modifying enrollments, or doing some other set of mundane tasks not in keeping with anything within my soul.

Alone, I drove about twenty-five miles from my house. I spent the day walking and hiking through woods unfamiliar to me. There I decided I would develop a plan to leave my job. While a wonderful job for someone, it was killing me. My day of aloneness proved to be a wonderful gift to myself as in just a few months, I turned my plans into reality.

While it can take a bit more effort to find it sometimes, self-love can be a magnificent gift, one that keeps on giving to us and others.

Time spent working and living in Pakistan provided exciting and rewarding unlimited learning experiences. Later, the coordinator of one of the programs there came with his beautiful and charming family to the US as part of his Fulbright program. As they departed, Shahid's wife, Rubina (as Ruby's friends and family call her) gave me a gorgeous ruby ring with diamonds on either side of it. I was so stunned I could hardly accept it. As I write this, it rests on my right hand. I wear it only in places where I know I and it will be safe. How I return it to Ruby's daughters I know not, but I want to be sure it gets back to her and her family. A gift of love that I've enjoyed in so many locations.

Another gift ring I guard just as jealously is a yellow gold and light jade one with initials inscribed. They were inscribed in Hong Kong by a woman named Betty when she bought and gave it to George, my former colleague, mentor, and friend. They were traveling, and it was a bonding time for them. George, more like a father to me than any other man, given that my own father died when I was seven, always had the gift of time for me and for others.

George's major gift to me was his caring and concern about me and my life. He was the one man, among many with whom I worked in an urban school district's central administration office, who believed and acted on the idea that women and minorities are as competent and effective as old white men his age. Through the years, he and I shared experiences with our various relationships—he as his wife died and he re-entered the dating scene, bringing a series of women past me to ascertain my observations of them, and I could let my tears flow, telling him of my fleeting relationship possibilities.

After George died, his daughter gave me the ring that Betty, one of the women with whom he shared some years before she passed away, had given to him. I had always admired it on his hand and now wear it frequently, always thinking of both of them and the gifts they gave to me. Kathy, his daughter, has continued his loving and giving manner as she quilts and cooks, sharing her loving attitude in so many ways.

The quilt she gave to me, a tribute to her father, is among her gifts, but none was as heartwarming as the one she gave years later when I felt lonely and distant from anyone. An email from her confirmed my request to visit her and her equally energetic husband. I was welcome to visit, they replied.

If George were still alive, I would have called him and arranged a visit. In his cozy family room, in front of his used brick fireplace and with books and magazines stacked on end tables, we would have set the world straight, discussing everything from our respective errant love lives to the world stage. When he was no longer available, his daughter welcomed me to her comfortable bungalow in Long Island, Washington. I just wanted to be with her and her husband. I wanted to stand in their gleaming white kitchen and see the decades of books where they had recorded details, including guests, of every meal they had catered. I wanted to see the sun coming through the specifically designed wall that showcased John's dazzling collection of glass ice buckets. I didn't need to stay long. Having the gift of their presence for a brief time was what I wanted, even needed. I went on my way, happy and content and grateful to them for the gift of their time, energy, and spirit.

On a friend's wall hangs a smiling photo of me, sun shining through my hair as I smile at the camera, holding a brilliant pink bougainvillea bouquet in my hand. I am trying to look my best, out of place as I am in my black all-purpose travel dress and reversible quilted cotton floral jacket. I know how to smile for the camera in settings like that, the ones where I, the foreigner, usually the only American, am paraded past locals whose lives are, on the surface, as different from mine as could possibly be. In this central India setting, my life and the locals are very different as many of these Indian villagers were afflicted years ago with leprosy. In this case, the villagers are accustomed to meeting foreigners, but often when I have traveled, I'm the first foreigner they have seen in person and likely the only one who will smile in their direction or shake hands with them.

The brilliant, bright pink bougainvillea had been given to me just a few dusty steps earlier by a tiny gray-haired woman, a foot shorter than me. She, a leper, had been in this leprosy community in India for most of her life, but she appeared happy to receive me and the group I had come with. I cradled the flowers, almost as I would a baby or as a Miss Universe might clutch floral bouquets after her win. I appreciated them, but I knew I did not know what I would do with them any more than I would a baby or as the beauty pageant winner would know what to do with her gift of flowers. I had no vase, no table to hold them. I had no one around me to whom I could ask to hold them.

But in that moment her gift touched me. This tiny, wizened woman, who owned little beyond her sari, knew how to give. She prepared her food on her minuscule stove in the communal kitchen and her memories gave her sufficient abundance whereby she could break off a small branch of stunning flowers and give them to me. To me! Someone she had never seen until a few minutes ago and would never see again after the short weeks I would live and work in the leprosy community. How honored and grateful I am.

Years later the leper's floral gift and its meaning remain with me. She is never forgotten in my heart, and I am grateful for the love she shared, one far greater than any I could have extended.

Many people, especially women, love to shop. Happily, they can spend hours poring over catalogs, watching television shopping channels, or strolling from one shop to another.

Not me. I confess I want the groceries to be on my shelves and my clothes to be in my closet, but I don't want to have to do the work to get them there. I'll pretty much make do with what I find on shelves and hangers if I can avoid going online or in person to a store.

Sometimes that makes me a magnet for friends to give their leftovers to me. And usually, I take them, especially when they come from friends who see shopping as a God-given responsibility. One of the world's best shoppers is my friend Kim.

Kim loves to shop. Her closets are bursting. Metal attachments have been added to wooden doors, creating additional space for hanging dresses and scarves. And then there's her black closet. That's the one she uses most frequently. Fifty pairs of every sort imaginable— black pants, black shirts, and black dresses hang. Black is the color she wears most often.

She's model thin with perfect skin and gorgeous long hair and can wear anything but usually chooses black. And black is perfect for her.

The little black dress did not come to fame for no good reason. Black is simple, basic, and easy. Any color, even brown, can match nicely with it. Black doesn't show dirt easily, unless it is scattered with white powder like our grandmothers used to wear. If black was good enough for Steve Jobs, it is good enough for me. Elizabeth Holmes, Theranos disgraced founder, nearly ruined the image, but it will prevail.

Through the years I have been the recipient of Kim's black largess. By that I mean that she has given me innumerable black pants, at least three of which I still own. As she gave them to me, I discovered that I, too, like wearing black. Fretting a bit, but not too much, about what others would think, I did wonder if they surmised that I thought black dealt me a slimmer look and one I needed. Perhaps I did need it and, possibly, it did "thin" me, but as I reviewed my behavior several times, I concluded I simply liked the way I felt when I wore black. Another example of a gift changing a wardrobe, even a life.

A royal blue, tightly woven nylon wooden handle handbag was the first gift I received from someone outside the US. My husband at the time and I were doing a summer's worth of missionary duty in Barbados. Not a bad place to be a missionary or do anything, right?

Jacarandas, bougainvillea, and breadfruit trees surrounded our broken glass-topped, walled-in compound. An open window from the second-floor kitchen allowed us to throw leftover food garbage out the window whereby it fell to a gutter below. From there it trickled along the street side gutter and went who knows where. The missionary supervisor allowed us to visit the locals' houses, but we were not allowed to invite them to our residence, a policy that did not set well with either me or my husband.

Some time that summer, among the wonderful Barbadian people we met who tolerated our cultural ignorance and taught us far more than we could have shared with them, a small, thin older woman presented me with the handbag. I didn't know what to do with it, its dark wooden handles constructed in the form of a fish, perfect for an island setting. Using hours of her own labor and energy, she had perfected the macrame handbag, lining it with the same rich color cotton.

Macrame consumes time and focus as the lacelike hand-knotted work done with strands of nylon, cotton, and jute form a wall-hanging, bag, dress, or other product. Macrame went out of style, at least where I lived. Decades later, languishing in my closet and having been moved to multiple states, I donated the bag. I can only hope that somewhere, someone is using the beautiful bag, but more so, I hope that the woman who gave it to me so long ago has lived a good life and can feel the energy of gratitude I feel toward her.

Years later, as television cameras rolled and I appeared, along with others from the Karachi, Pakistan university where my international colleagues and I were teaching management, the Sindh governor presented me with yards of fabric. An unusual gift by American standards, a perfect one by Pakistani culture. Fabric stores there abound, each presenting different and gorgeous offerings. Women rarely purchase an outfit from a rack but are accustomed to having a tailor, working cross-legged in cramped quarters, make clothes to their design and fabric choice. Those planning to migrate might save their fabric for years, taking it with them when they move, not too different from what I have done. Now the yards wrap a blanket, matching its bright colors with my red couch in Mexico.

The handsome leader likely gave a different kind of gift to the men in the group, maybe even none at all. I recall not. I only know that the bright yards of dark yellow floral thin cotton he gave me are beautiful. They remain unused, aside from wrapping the blanket, because anything I think of having sewn with the fabric seems unworthy of its memory. A tablecloth, perhaps, I say. Ahh, not quite right. Maybe a dress. No. There's too much fabric, and then what would I do with the rest of it? It could be wasted, and it is far too precious to allow that to happen. It isn't the financial value of the fabric that makes it so precious. It is the memory of my time and experience with my Karachi colleagues and students that make the fabric far too precious to consider wasting.

Sometime, yes, sometime, the perfect idea will come to me for how to best use the fabric. Or, I will give it to someone, sharing the history of the fabric, hoping it will create a beautiful memory for them.

Writing this, I think of a former boyfriend's mother's gifts. Both small, elegant, and tasteful, I cherish them as I did the short time we spent together. The gifts remind me of her and her kindnesses toward me. I wish we could have spent much more time together as I would liked to have heard the stories I am sure she had.

Too often we forget the gifts our parents or guardians have given to us. Some they gave to us by design. Others, they gave unknowingly. Although her budget was extremely limited, I'm sure my mother gave me various gifts through the years. I don't remember all of them, but what I do recall is the time and she spent with me. Winter evenings we spent huddled together playing word games. Summers, she threw baseballs to me so that when I played with other children, I would have some idea how to hold the bat or to catch the ball. A perfect gift for a child with no near-age siblings or nearby playmates.

The basketball hoop installed for my eleventh birthday, something no other girl my age I knew owned, was surely the prize gift I received from her. Stationed near our garage and adjacent to the field Mother rented to local farmers, the hoop was used by no one except Mother and me. Of all the objects she might have given me, I now wonder what inspired her, aside from me asking, to give me the gift. I was not an athletic child, preferring to keep my nose planted firmly in books. It may not have increased my basketball playing skills, but it did increase my praying that my local high school team would win.

What was the best gift my mother gave to me? Independence. While guiding and keeping a motherly eye on me, she let me develop my own wings, gaining independence, not squashing any creativity or initiative I had. Letting me fall and fail sometimes, all the while, letting me develop into who I would become was a huge gift in my life. Stifling me would not have been productive for either of us.

Gourmet editor and food writer Ruth Reichl says her mother trained her to be defiant, a worthy skill in many areas. I can't say that my mother instilled defiance in me but independence, yes.

To Think About

1. What's the absolutely best gift anyone, including yourself, has ever given to you? What was the result?

2. If you were looking for a best gift now for yourself, what would it be? Does this gift differ from one you might have asked for earlier? How did you conclude this would be the BEST gift?

84

3. What gift has been given to you that was wrapped in a way that surprised you, and how did it surprise you? Did it make you think differently about the giver, the gift, or yourself?

Giving as Strategy

You cannot receive what you don't give. Outflow determines inflow.

—Eckhart Tolle

*I*N ASTANA, RENAMED NUR-SULTAN WHEN Kazakhstan's first president left office, I visited the President's Center of Culture and Museum. Wearing disposable, white shoe coverings as I passed historical objects including jewelry, I viewed showcases of items given to President Nursultan Nazarbayev. Included among them were gifts from the forty-second president of the United States, Bill Clinton.

The Office of the Federal Register catalogs every gift that US presidents and those connected to them receive, including a note about the gift's value and any relevant information. Not accepting the gifts, even one of the 15,000 given each year would cause embarrassment for the US. President Clinton and other presidents, beginning with George Washington, received numerous gifts of state, many of which can be seen in various museums, making the process one related to international diplomacy. Occasionally personal, usually such gifts have some sentiment or show of connection between the two countries.

The US has a specific department focused on gift giving, the Office of Protocol Gift Unit. What this office, Donald Rumsfeld, or his staff were thinking when they gave Iraq's Saddam Hussein spiked torture hammers, one can hardly imagine. Diplomatic gifts are usually intended in some way to put the receiver in the giver's debt. The same is true in business.

Starting my business years ago, I ran into numerous unforeseen challenges. Eventually they worked out to my benefit; meanwhile, every day of my life was filled with agony and stress. An acquaintance, one I thought was in the process of becoming a friend, gave me several gifts for which I felt uncomfortable. I appreciated them and thanked her; however, in my naivete, it never occurred to me that she was engaging in a gift giving strategy. I discovered that she wanted me to hire her for a job with the company when I won a major albeit troublesome contract. The gift giving was not because she liked or admired me but because she wanted something in return, something I chose not to give.

More recently, we read gift giving stories that include human beings "given" to other humans for ill use. Sex and labor trafficking falls into that category. Parents giving their children for ill-begotten gains. Men giving their wives to another man for sexual purposes as if the wife were a lawn mower or electric drill that could be given or loaned in exchange for another item has occurred too frequently. Equal value here has no place in such a conversation.

Some businesspeople are accustomed to giving and receiving gifts as part of a strategy or a tactic to win and keep new and old clients.

A decade ago, in the steamy heat of an auditorium in Shanghai's outskirts, standing with my university colleagues while its president presented an honorary doctorate to one of China's wealthiest men, I saw gift giving strategy in action. Thin skinned, wrinkled old men lined up in the front row would have lived through the horrendous Tiananmen Square times, perhaps even creating or partaking in them. The recipient, a father of four children had made his money from a large, well known, multi-level marketing scheme selling health and home products in China. While the handsome recipient appeared to be a pleasant enough man, I wondered what he had done in the way of scholarship that made him appropriate to receive the honorary doctorate.

This was the second honorary doctorate we had awarded in similar fashion. An earlier one had been given to one of the country's congressional members. The exact exchange the university would receive for the gift we would never know, but it likely included access to China's higher state and national government as well as to other business leaders. A useful investment for the gift of paper and accompanying hoopla. After all, the university was not just a place of learning. For its president, it was a business for him and his family.

Similar arrangements occur within the US as

honorary doctorates, awards, and accolades are given by organizations in exchange for access to political figures, information, or something else.

Records indicate that President Thomas Jefferson had a firm policy of not accepting gifts from foreigners; however, he wavered and gave in when the Tunisian ambassador presented him with four Arabian horses. He maintained that his justification was that he could sell the horses, thereby offsetting the cost of the ambassador's visit. Little evidence appears to exist as to what actually happened to the horses.

The Dalai Lama has said that the best gift anyone could give him for his eighty-fifth birthday is to "do some good and kind work to help others." Likely a good gift for any year or anyone. No gift wrapping needed and regifting is easy.

Gifts of the Sultan: The Arts of Giving at the Islamic Courts, edited by Linda Komaroff, highlights gift exchanges in western Europe and eastern Asia. Not too different from what we see in current times with gift exchanges between US presidents and Mideast leaders, all given for various purposes but intended to strengthen relationships between the countries and regions. Do they make a difference these days? Who knows? But I would opine that it is unlikely that they have much impact on policy development outcomes.

While I think they make no difference, I do not know that with complete confidence. Perhaps a ruler looking at a gift received learns more about the meaning of the gift, then takes action while never sharing the thoughts or decision-making process. Rarely do we know the ultimate impact of our gifts.

To Think About

1. Have you ever given a gift in anticipation of how it might benefit you? If so, how did that work out for you? Would your actions be different now?

2. Have you been given a gift that you felt was given to you only in anticipation of what you might provide to the giver? Did it make you think differently about the gift or the giver? Did your thoughts change about the event as time passed?

Unwanted Gifts I Have Received and Given

Age has given me the gift of me.

—Anne Lamott

EVEN THE FUTURE KING OF ENGLAND CAN HAVE some difficulty with gift giving. Recently, Prince William shared with the public how he found himself in an awkward situation when he gave his wife, Kate Middleton, a pair of binoculars when they were courting. She did not receive the gift as he expected, asking, "what's going on"? I confess if I had been advising him, definitely an unlikely possibility, I would have suggested binoculars as an outstanding idea. After all, she likes sports and could use them to see soccer, polo, or other sports at closer range. She likes the country, so bird watching would be easier with binoculars. On and on, but again, what success have I had with gift giving?

Occasionally . . . probably more than occasionally, I have been given an item that I did not want. Bringing a gift meant that someone had spent some time thinking about what I might want or need, or at least their perception of it. They had gone to some trouble to acquire it and then put it in a form to present to me. Now I was charged with what to do with it.

One year I received a gift from a friend. The gift was the same one I had given her two years previously. That she had not used it or enjoyed it make me even more shy about searching for a gift for her. On the other hand, I could have used a gift journal, one that would have kept me from giving the same silver-plated table crumb brush to my boss. My lesson there was that people can be forgiving. He and his wife continued to be kind and loving toward me, incompetent as I might have been in the gift giving arena.

Comedian Craig Ferguson said the worst gift he ever received when he got out of rehab was a bottle of wine. He went on to say the wine was delicious, clearly his way of saying the gift was not the most appropriate or what he wanted or needed at that particular time in his life.

A graduate studies colleague, one whom I barely knew, once showed up at my office with a plant gift in hand for me. Considered a bit unusual by most of the other students, she had chosen a gift that matched how they perceived her. Why she chose to give it to me, I will never know. And I still do not know the name or origin of the plant, despite efforts to discover a likeness.

We were studying in Oregon and she was from Tennessee, so it seemed unlikely that a tropical plant had been grown in either a nearby backyard or a greenhouse. Resembling a Proteus Pinwheel, also known as Catherine-wheel Pincushion, the light greenish stalk held the potential for a bloom, but how it would look, I could hardly imagine. It seemed eerie, more like an animal in a grizzled, twisted decomposing state. Puzzled, I thanked her and went on about my studies. A few weeks later she asked if I would take her to the grocery to get wine for a student departmental party. Given I was one of the student representatives and one who had a car, even a new one, I felt obligated to give her a lift. By the time we finished the errand, she had allowed a gallon jug of red wine to break, liquid running the length of the car. I recall few to no apologies or offers to clean or repair the smelly and badly stained carpet.

While this gift giving experience rarely returns to my mind, when it does, I confess I have not yet discovered the meaning, even the value of it. Perhaps one day. Maybe one does not need to find meaning in every action, including gift giving.

When I first moved to my house in the California countryside, I discovered a chicken coop. Not one to want anything to be wasted, I made a deal with the guest house tenant. I'd purchase the chickens and feed for them if she would take care of them, an arrangement that worked for both of us.

At my corporate job, I hired Sandra, one of several employees to support completing a fast-moving project. She and I discovered we had some common experiences and interests. She was low on funds and struggling to make ends meet.

My chickens were producing more eggs than I could possibly consume. Often, I took dozens to the local women's shelter. One day when Sandra was coming to visit, I grabbed an empty egg carton, gathered eggs directly from the nests, put them into the carton ready to give to her. She arrived and I presented them to her, thinking that while it was not a huge gift, she would be pleased to receive some free-range chicken eggs.

She appeared cool to the gift, barely thanking me for them. Only much later did I realize that it was likely that she had never seen eggs of mismatched sizes or with a tiny bit of chicken feces on some of the eggs. Such didn't bother me. I had not thought of washing them before I gave them to her given that eggs are broken and dumped into a dish or pan before cooking, never being affected by the shell's exterior. Or that she could wash them easily. So much for my gift giving success.

As years have passed, she probably has told others of the appalling gift I gave to her. We have lost track of one another, and I have been unable to find her online, so it is unlikely I will ever know. I can only hope it inspired her to learn about organic eggs, environmental issues, methods for creating outstanding French omelets, or something else that has brought great happiness to her.

Another so-called gift I gave that was not the best choice occurred high in the Pakistani Pir Panjal mountain range. Grateful for the experience of teaching management and marketing to some of the brightest undergraduate and graduate students I have had the opportunity to encounter, I wanted to explore as much as I could of their fascinating and beautiful country. Each weekend I taxied to the bus station, bought a ticket, and headed out to discover as much as I could. On one such trip, I wanted to explore Murree, the mountain resort town northeast of the country's capital. When the region had been part of India, British officers and their families often sought Murree for its beauty and, in the summer, for its cool air, far different from Delhi's stifling heat.

Like bus companies in many countries, the organization provided a small packaged lunch that included fruit, a sweet, and a sandwich on white bread. I can eat and have eaten just about anything. However, one of the items on my least liked list is plain, soft, almost gooey white bread. Furthermore, the sack lunch was too much like something I might have been given as a lunch when I was in elementary school. Besides, I was in Pakistan. I wanted real Pakistani food—flavorful biryani or a spicy kabob.

I arrived, found a guest house, and with my untouched sack lunch still in my day pack, I set out for a walk. As I sauntered around town, checking out meat stalls, vegetable bins, tiny clothing outlets, I saw a bedraggled elderly man wearing a dirty *shalwar chameez*, extending his hand in a begging mannerism, looking hungry and thin. I remembered my lunch sack.

I stepped off the main path, dug into my pack, finding the untouched, white lunch sack containing the offending white bread and other items. I dug it out, thinking that while the food did not appeal to me, perhaps he would find it nourishing.

"As-Salamu Alaykum," I greeted him. "Peace be upon you", I said. Quietly greeting me in return, he stared at me. Unlikely that he had seen a lot of blond-haired women in western dress. I had become accustomed to the stares, so I thought little of his non-responsiveness. I handed him the package of my unused lunch. Placing my right hand

over my heart, I bowed slightly to him and handed him the lunch gift, then turned and walked away.

At a distance I turned, watching him looking puzzled as he opened the lunch sack. Then I saw him shake his head in disappointment. Perhaps he did not like plain white bread sandwiches any more than I did. Likely he would have preferred a gift of Pakistani rupees.

I will never know what impact the gift made on the old man. Did any disdain he had for foreigners or women or anyone only increase due to the gift? Did he later find nourishment in the food? Did he regift the items, perhaps to a waiting donkey?

To Think About

1. Have you ever received a gift you did not want? What did you do when you received it?

2. What have you done with unwanted gifts? Would you take the same action again?

Gifts: Routes to Learning

*Every problem is a gift—without
problems we would not grow.*

—Anthony Robbins

A FRIEND AND COLLEAGUE, ONE WHO LEFT THIS
life far too soon due to ovarian cancer, once
surprised me with a gift, a book. That she gave
me a book was not surprising given both of us were
avid readers. It was this book's cover and its contents
that surprised me.

Falkland Road: Prostitutes of Bombay, written by
photographer Mary Ellen Mark, showed a young, dark-
skinned girl, breasts displayed, on the book's cover. I
looked at the naked, childlike Indian woman wearing
only an ornate necklace dangling between her breasts.
I began to learn about a part of women's lives, so foreign
from my own. I'd never thought much about prostitutes.
I didn't judge or blame them for their occupational
activity, but I had no connection to them. While I didn't
aspire to be one, sometimes I wondered if I had become

an intellectual prostitute as I labored in jobs I did not enjoy or appreciate.

Although I'd been in Bombay, now called Mumbai, numerous times, I'd never been to Falkland Road. I knew little about prostitutes in India or elsewhere. Yet, as I read about the women who worked in the sex industry there, it increased my interest in learning more about the culture of India.

Gifts given to Mumbai prostitutes are rare. When given, usually they are to encourage the sex workers to entice more potential victims so their pimps, or maliks as they would be called there, could make more money. Servicing no less than twenty men a day, acquiring money from the prostitutes for their lodging, food, and other made-up essentials, could provide an uncaring man a sufficient income for little real effort. Likely all the waters of the sacred Ganges can never wash away the agony these young women experience.

I'd been interested in India since I read about a missionary whose last name was the same as mine. I was in the third grade, reading a Sunday School magazine. Older, I continued to be on alert when anything about India was mentioned, even being mesmerized by a handsome, khaki-suit-wearing, pink-turbaned man crossing a San Francisco street. As I turned to admire him, I saw him returning the stare.

"Our grandmother is Indian," my sister told me more than once. I thought she meant Indian as in Native American. Yes, the only photo I had seen of our grandmother showed a dark-skinned woman with black hair curling slightly as it circled her face. Two of my nephews could pass for citizens from the Indian subcontinent given the right haircut and dressed in a *shalwar kameez,* but nothing else in my background spoke to any cultural difference from a basic white, Anglo-Saxon history.

Then a cousin gave me a copy of my father's mother's birth certificate. Her middle names were East India. Born in 1870, she was not eligible for a hippie name like Sky, Rainbow, or Harmony. Why my grandmother's parents, with commonly known last names and a first name popular through the centuries for young women, chose to insert East India into her name, I will never know. Genealogical research I have done has provided no clues as to why and how this might have happened, but it provides a gift that ties me to India.

My mother's gift to a teenage me of a Frank Sinatra album plus one of Beethoven's Fifth Symphony started me on a lifetime of appreciating crooner and classical music. Often, as she retired to bed in the evenings, I would lie on the couch, feet up on its back, dreaming about how my life would be. No, it has not turned out that I have had a grand piano sitting on a white carpeted step-down living room in the Manhattan apartment that I dreamed about, but I have had three houses with white carpeting, a grand piano, and a terrace that I refer to as the Manhattan deck, given it overlooks a beautiful city. I recall her gift with kindness, acknowledge the many ways it shaped parts of my life.

Ahhh, the routes that gifts can take us, physically and in our minds.

To Think About

1. Have you received any gifts, tangible or intangible, that led you to learn a new skill or a new way of thinking about a topic?

2. Can you think of people, especially young ones, to whom you could give a gift that might encourage their learning?

Regifting

Practice giving things away, not just things you don't care about, but things you do like.

—Huston Smith

REGIFTING HAS RECEIVED A LOT OF DISCUSSION IN the last couple of decades. While I am unopposed to it, I know I've been the recipient. Once I received a gift from a friend that I had given her two years previously. Another time I gave my boss and his wife the same gift two times in a row, not exactly the same item as both times I had purchased the gifts new. Embarrassing? Absolutely.

An online list says that candles are the most frequently regifted item, followed by related houseware products. A couple of decades ago, late-night comedian Johnny Carson suggested only one fruitcake existed in the world and that it was regifted from one person to another, year after year. Perhaps for that reason, fruitcakes around winter holiday periods are much more difficult to find in

American stores these days than they were a few years ago.

Some oppose regifting, believing it is bad luck as it gives away friendship. As difficult as it is to find a gift one's beloved colleagues or relatives will use and enjoy, it seems reasonable to regift if appropriate. And it forestalls the item ending in the landfill, a worthy cause for all.

Regifting proponents have developed a whole set of rules, telling the giver what they should and should not do. I'll spare you reading them here as they are available online, but I do suggest you may want to skim them before your gift giving event is about to occur.

No, I don't want to receive a zero-balance gift card, expired software, or monogrammed items with someone else's initials. And neither does anyone else.

 ## To Think About

1. Have you received a gift that you know had been given to the person who gave it to you? How did you feel about that then and now? Are there any differences?

Giving What You Have

Time, as far as my father was concerned,
was a gift you gave to other people.

— Michelle Obama, *Becoming*

YOU MAY THINK, ESPECIALLY AFTER THE PANDEMIC, you have so little money that you can give nothing to anyone, certainly not anyone who has more financial resources than you. You say you are not the kind of person who would want to give or receive one of those cutesy cards awarding the recipient a home-cooked dinner, a foot massage, or their equivalent.

That's fine. I understand.

Recently, a friend forwarded me the obituary of her colleague's 102-year-old mother. The mother had been loved by many people in her community, having lived in the same southern California location throughout her entire life. On her one hundredth birthday she shared an unnoticed gift she had received as she said, "Living in the same place has not prevented me from experiencing the world's cultures. I have been blessed to have the world come to me through my friends." A gift of a different sort but one that allowed her to give to others in a way she may not otherwise have done.

Maybe you don't have to give anything to those who have more financial resources than you. Perhaps your gifting can be to someone you barely know, maybe have not even met. Also, it could be that giving your listening skills, merely your being present with that other person, or your verbal or nonverbal encouragement can become your gift to them.

Not always do recipients need to know they are being given a gift. Only years later will they have their "aha" moment, recalling the beauty and deep feelings the gift provided them. And you may never know if they really "received" your gift. Your job is only to give, not to hang around waiting for thanks, in whatever form you might hope it would come.

Just give.

Then give yourself a gift of letting go of your angst and loving you for being your best self.

To Think About

1. To whom would you like to give something, if you could? Would it be a tangible or intangible item?

2. What keeps you from giving it to them? Is there another way to think about it?

3. What do you think might happen if you gave it to them?

Receiving When You Were Not Ready

I'm cursed with the gift of foresight.

—Morrissey

TAKE A MINUTE AND THINK ABOUT THIS. WERE YOU given hand-me-downs as a child, ones that embarrassed you when you had to wear them to school as they fit but were outdated? What about the time your boyfriend proposed, holding a ring in his hand that was so tiny and ugly you could hardly imagine wearing it to a party, much less for the rest of your life?

What have you been given that you did not want? What about gifts you were given that you did not want but later, perhaps even now, you think you could not live without?

Like birds engaged in mating dance rituals, often men are fervent gift givers. As I began this paragraph, the man with whom I have been living brought me a pair of binoculars, perhaps so I can watch birds as I write. Earlier, he, an excellent cook, had brought a delicious bowl of eggs and chorizo for breakfast. I wanted neither the binoculars nor the eggs, wanting only the beauty of the rooftop garden and the quiet to write, but I appreciated both. Knowing he was returning downstairs to the kitchen, I asked if he would be willing to take down the nearly empty egg dish.

"I'm not your servant," he snarled.

Whoops, I thought. One thing at a time. Accept a gift. Thank the person. Later, ask, even if it is less efficient, for the favor, but do it later.

Timing remains everything—in gift giving and gift receiving.

I confess I've been snippy about gifts. Perhaps my concern about items relocating to the landfill because they were not used overtook my sensitivity about the other person's feelings. I've returned a ring and a watch to a man as they were not ones that I knew I'd be comfortable wearing. I've even complained about a gift of Bert's Bees products. How petty could I be, you wonder. Now you know. Don't judge. You may have your own list.

As I reflect on gifts I've received through the years, the elaborately printed Indian pillbox, the sage hooded and pocketed long fleece robe, the black and colored striped beach bag, and numerous other ones, I recall my reaction when I received them. Why was I being given this item? That seemed to be my first thought. I didn't seem to know what to do with the gift and maybe, if I didn't know what to do with it, I shouldn't have been given it. Did I think it was too good for me, that I was undeserving? Did I not like the item? Certainly, in the case of the above-mentioned items, that was not true. I liked the items, even more as time has passed. The pillbox has traveled the world with me, and the robe became an all-time favorite item, perfect for curling up in on chilly evenings. Worn thin now from countless launderings, it will become the pattern for a new one. Sounds to me like a pretty good gift-receiver match.

Did I feel beholden to the giver? Perhaps. As I dig a little deeper into my memories of my feelings at the receiving time, perhaps I felt that I'd never be able to give the giver a gift as wonderful as the one they presented to me.

I did not think the gift giver expected anything from me. Any thought like that was more of me projecting an untruth onto the giver. In reality, gifts are often given with no expectation, little more than an acknowledgment of it. A spoken, or even better, a hand-written thank you makes it all the better. However, if the giver is intent on receiving such, likely they should not be in the giving business.

I'm appreciative of when my Mexican neighbor hands me a jar full of flavorful beans, a kind I've never seen. It gives me joy but not nearly as much as when I've made a cheesecake or vegetable soup, leaving the container on his doorstep or handing it to him through the patio. I can only hope he enjoys these food gifts. If not, they will go into the compost pile or over the wall where waiting possums will feast that evening, a gift for them. Gifts can keep on giving in multiple locations and situations, wanted or not.

To Think About

1. Have you ever received a gift that you thought was given to you with ulterior motives? Did you feel you needed to respond in a certain way?

2. Have you ever given a gift with ulterior motives? What were those motives?

Wishing for Gifts You Wish You Received or Gave

Adulthood is not a goal. It's not seen as a gift.

—Frances McDormand

*A*S I'VE WRITTEN HERE, GIFT GIVING IS EASY FOR some but not for others, like me. It can be a chore that we would like to accomplish, moving on to other activities we enjoy more. For those of us in the latter category, too often we can make mistakes in our gift choices, thereby creating hard feelings from the receiver.

At other times, regardless of what gift we choose, the receiver can take umbrage, being miffed at our best intentions. That great T-shirt we thought Aunt Sherilyn would love? Oh, no! What made her think I wear anything that big...or that small...or that color...or with/without that logo? The software game we gave to Cousin Brett's children? Outdated, they say, not bothering to unwrap the box.

I or someone else can provide do and do-not lists for what one should or should not give. I refrain from that here. However, I encourage you to think beyond your usual seat-of-the-skirt/pants thought processes as you plan your gifts. Because someone has a collection of chicken tchotchkes, don't assume they want another one of Garrison Keillor's Lake Woebegone characters. Being a fan of born-again religious writing does not mean they would welcome a book by the Dali Lama or Sufism and the reverse.

Consider if your gift is going to create additional work that the receiver may not want to have to perform, either themselves or by hiring someone else. Yes, your father may have longed for a train set. You are excited that now you have the funds to provide that gift for him; however, does he have the space for it, especially if he is planning on downsizing next year to a retirement community? Is he able to assemble it himself? Would other household members, complaining about the train's whistle as it circles the track, bring more grief than enjoyment to him? Maybe a subscription to a model train magazine or train ticket would suffice.

As I write this, I ponder what gifts I wish I had been given. It is easy to say that I, we, any of us would like to have received a huge financial inheritance, never considering the challenges that such might bring. Jealousy from relatives or peers, never-ending legal and bookkeeping efforts to retain or grow the inheritance can cause loss of sleep. Guilt about our behavior to the gift giver might arise. On and on.

When I think more deeply about what gifts I would like to have received, probably I would put encouragement at the top of the list. I wish more professors, bosses, colleagues would have encouraged me to think bigger, try harder, be more. I am the kind of personality that responds to encouragement; positive statements increase my self-esteem. Perhaps others do not. Maybe along with that, I am saying I wish I had received more praise for what I did or that someone could have guided me to doing what I did in a better way. I was working hard but was the energy directed to my best life?

As years have passed, I have discovered that while I may not have received as much encouragement and support as I wished, I can give support to others. I cannot encourage others when it is not in their best interest or when their desired talents are not present. Only when I can be honest is the gift an appropriate one, but oh, the joy it brings when I can provide that support, that encouragement that moves them on to their goals.

Possibly, the lack of encouragement and praise was the better gift, the one that kept me "hungry," independent, learning to accept what my life presented while challenging myself forward. Maybe I've been learning how to give myself and others' gifts. Encouragement and praise are ones I can give myself, but I want to give them to others when appropriate.

I could wish I had not given a friend an undersink composter, given I know she has never used it. Perhaps my gift, while she did not use it, has increased her awareness of environmental issues. Maybe she has found another worthy purpose for it or she was able to give it to someone else, creating yet another learning situation.

The Zoomie glasses with built-in binoculars? Doesn't everyone need a pair?

I do not know about that gift, a crazy one, given to a couple of friends. At the time I was searching for gifts for them, the crazy glasses seemed like fun and would make them unique among others in their social settings. No, they probably would not and did not wear them often, and yes, they probably will end their life in a landfill. Meanwhile, I had found a fun gift for them and one of which they remind me occasionally—the big visor hats I got for them when I worked in China. Right along with the Zoomie binoculars, they say.

Did I buy these for myself? No. Somehow, I didn't think it appropriate, necessary, reasonable. I do not know what the right adjective would be. I just know I have learned that often, gifts I would give to others were not ones I deemed myself appropriate to have. Hmmm. A potential lesson for me there, it would seem.

Time to reflect on what I have not given myself. Perhaps I have not wanted the items or the experiences enough. Maybe I had only a fleeting desire for them, not enough to encourage me to take action about them. Perhaps the timing has not been correct, that I am not ready to manage whatever might accompany the item or experience. For example, maybe I want a swimming pool but am I ready for the maintenance, fear of someone drowning in it, the upheaval of workers adding it to my property, the guilt of not inviting others to join me on hot days, of adding solar systems to heat the water to the temperature I prefer? On and on.

Poet and novelist May Sarton wrote in *Journal of a Solitude* that even though she had many people to surround her whom she loved, to be without solitude was more challenging that any of the issues related to that activity, A gift, I would say, she gave to herself. Too often we feel guilty about giving to ourselves the very gifts we want most, the ones that would add, ultimately, to our and others' lives in positive ways.

To Think About

1. What kinds of gifts do you usually give? Is there a pattern?

2. Do you typically search for humorous, silly gifts? Do you choose practical gifts, ones that can be used numerous times? Do you choose gifts whereby the receiver will learn a new skill, behavior, or attitude? Do you give gifts that no one else will give the receiver or ones that are common to the person's age, class, gender, culture, education, or other common characteristic?

3. Do you search relentlessly for gifts or give what is easy to find?

4. What kinds of gifts do you like to receive? For example, do you like practical gifts, homemade gifts, expensive and elegantly wrapped gifts? Do you prefer gift cards?

5. Do you prefer to receive what you have asked for or do you like to be surprised by gifts?

Wrapping Up...

*A*S I NEARED FINISHING THIS BOOK, ANOTHER GIFT experience, one I'll be remembering for a long time, occurred.

I, like others around the world, was pretty much shuttered, even cloistered, for several months during the pandemic. As San Miguel de Allende, the historic, beautiful, colonial town where I've been spending pandemic time re-opened, I donned my mask, my face shield, and courage to walk its streets again. I disinfected my fingers, card, and money when I finished at the ATM, continuing on toward La Bibliotheca, the library that serves as a major meeting place for expats and Mexicans. I knew it would be closed but even walking past it would feel good to this bibliophile.

Nearing it, I saw that while the library, with its Spanish and English books, stunning murals, and wide, interior plaza, remained closed, its gift shop had open doors. I walked across the sanitation mat, extended my arm to the temperature taker, and signed in with the security guard. Sauntering through the Spanish and English books, I lingered. Were there any books I could not live without? Any gift items I should purchase? I shopped alone with only the security guard and the clerk among the beaded jewelry, embroidered cushion covers, hot pads, and books by local authors.

I returned to the used English book section when, to my right, a young, pleasant looking, small in stature man came up to me. Gently, he grabbed my hand, pressing into my palm a small object. Thinking it likely he was begging, and I would need to fumble through my bag to find pesos to give him, I checked my surroundings, assuring myself it was not a ruse to distract me whereby another person grabbed my bag. "*Gracias*, no," I said gently but firmly as he continued to hold my hand in both of his.

Inside my palm he had placed a heart-shaped red stone, perhaps plastic, surrounded by a perfectly crafted silver holding. On either side of the heart were two silver "holes" through which a chain could hold it in place.

"No," he said. "It is for you. You must have this," he insisted. With that, he closed my palm tighter, turned and moved quickly toward the exit and security guard where he picked up his three black bags, walked out the door, and vanished.

I stood, askance, staring at the doorway. The clerk came toward me as I said, "Who was that? Why did he give this to me?" Speaking to me in English, she said, "I do not know. Sometimes those things just happen. We never know why," as if the gift giving behavior were an almost common occurrence.

When I pulled myself together, knowing it unlikely I would ever see this man again, I thought of how, once more, I had been given an unexpected gift. I exited the gift shop, turned right, ambled down the old cobblestone streets, marveling at how the Universe works. Likely I will recall the event numerous times throughout my life. Also, likely, at some time in my life, I will meet the person to whom I will know I should regift this item, passing it on to them while telling them the story of how I received it. It will be a special person, one who is meant to receive it. Meanwhile, I accept it as an affirmation that while I am grateful for the gifts, including the red-trimmed in silver heart, this book will be a gift of love to others around the world. We must continue to give . . . and to receive.

To Think About

1. Keep giving... and receiving.

 **BARBARA COLE, PH.D.**, holds immense gratitude for numerous material and intangible gifts received working for a Fortune 500 company, owning her own testing and training company, and teaching management in the United States, throughout China, Ecuador, Kazakhstan, and Pakistan. Her work has appeared in *Still Point Arts Quarterly*, *Woods Reader* and other journals. She divides her time between Monterey, California, and San Miguel de Allende, Mexico.

SHANTI ARTS

NATURE · ART · SPIRIT

Please visit us online
to browse our entire book catalog,
including poetry collections and fiction,
books on travel, nature, healing, art,
photography, and more.

Also take a look at our highly regarded art
and literary journal, *Still Point Arts Quarterly*,
which may be downloaded for free.

www.shantiarts.com

CPSIA information can be obtained
at www.ICGtesting.com
Printed in the USA
BVHW042340140423
662364BV00012B/1227